Still Life with Rope and River

poems by

Chavonn Williams Shen

Finishing Line Press
Georgetown, Kentucky

Still Life with Rope and River

Copyright © 2024 by Chavonn Williams Shen
ISBN 979-8-88838-703-0 First Edition
All rights reserved under International and Pan-American Copyright Conventions. No part of this book may be reproduced in any manner whatsoever without written permission from the publisher, except in the case of brief quotations embodied in critical articles and reviews.

Publisher: Leah Huete de Maines
Editor: Christen Kincaid
Cover Art: Royce Galindo
Author Photo: Peter Limthongviratn
Cover Design: Elizabeth Maines McCleavy

Order online: www.finishinglinepress.com
also available on amazon.com

Author inquiries and mail orders:
Finishing Line Press
PO Box 1626
Georgetown, Kentucky 40324
USA

Contents

Author's Note	1
Legion	3
B.L. Mims	4
Walthall County, Mississippi	5
Ode to My Unkept Sobriety	6
The Slave's Descendant Addresses King Cotton	8
Ode to the Decrepit Auction Block Seen on the Way to My Grandfather's House	9
Milam and Bryant	10
Henry Lee Logins	11
Ode to the River As It Comes Undone	12
The Cotton Gin Recalls Emmett	13
A Concerned Citizen	14
Riddles in the Dark	15
Wheeler Parker	16
death's to-do list	17
Legion	18
No	19
The Jury	20
Press Release	21
Coon Hunting	23
The Noose Undone	24
"THE LAW: Trial by Jury"	25
Pike County, Mississippi	27
Inventory of a Black Girl	28
Legion	29
Trees (Noun)	30
Interview with Carolyn Bryant on the Anniversary of Emmett's Death	31
"The Shocking Story of Approved Killing in Mississippi"	33

Moses Wright 34
Jet Magazine Staff 35
"Historian Recalls Moment Emmett's Accuser Admitted She Lied" 36
To Be Soft.. 37
A Subtle Truth / Self Portrait as a Chair 38
4 40
The Train as Mother Speaks... 41
"Why Are We Still Reliving the Nightmarish Death of Emmett Till?" 42
The Only Black Kid at a Punk Show 44
Legion 45
Praise be the Planters 46
Repurposed Litany 47

Notes 49
Acknowledgments.. 51

Author's Note

"Emmett is dead. I don't know why he can't just stay dead."
—Roy Bryant

Too many stories aren't properly told. This is especially true with the death of Emmett Till. Narratives of those nights contradict and his death becomes more distant. Though many of the stories written here are imagined, their foundation is real. When the truth is inconvenient, it's replaced.

I am humbled by the storytellers who existed before me: Gwendolyn Brooks, Cornelius Eady, Tyehimba Jess, Lucille Clifton, and the legion of others that shifted through contradictions, made room for their own narratives, and wrote what's true.

Legion

They named us legion for we
are many. Some died soaked in sap
with halos of leaves. Some left no body
at all, only curses
to know we once were.

B. L. Mims

Me and my friend were fishing
when we saw something sticking out

of the water. I was hoping it was a big carp 'cause it was mighty hot
and we were catching

nothing. I went over to get a better look and I saw a head bobbing
about. I remember thinking it might a colored boy,

'cause I've seen with my own eyes what could happen if one of them
said the wrong thing to some white who was already vexed. It was
covered in so much

mud I couldn't it see it right. The body was so smashed up, I could
hardly imagine it alive in the first place.

Walthall County, Mississippi

I. *Ode to the Sidewalks that Lead to My Grandfather's House*

My father once told me
how his father often pushed him
into the street. No traffic to fear
in this small town, just white folk mad
that a Black boy almost brushed
the hems of their shirts.

II. *Ode to the Oak Near My Grandfather's House*

Its branches built for swinging,
rope wrapped round its boughs held
a cast off tire in place. Older cousins taught
those younger how to lean back before their feet met the grass.
How to twist the rope so tight
that heads spun with each release.

Ode to My Unkept Sobriety

O final drops

                                            earn my grave-scented mo

uth.

        Garnished

                                                    with glass

                    cure my blood

           of this hunger.

                    Smooth gold swirled

                                                in flutes make

              music

                    of these wounds.

O empty bottle

              lick my casket clean.

      Compose a litany of

clanking flasks.

          Divorce dirt

                from clenched fists.

      Build mountains

                                      near my stomach.

Keep me company.

Smell the earth   on my breath.

The Slave's Descendant Addresses King Cotton

You watch me harvest cotton
dresses from discount racks, pleased by my labor. You delight when I write
of my grandmother's hands and that time they tore like loose seams
after a day in the fields. You occupy my bed,
my shirts, my country's closets. Slaves would be shamed
to know their seed writes of them, wrapped in quilts
made from their sweat. Shamed to know I buy fresh sugarcane
because it tastes like home. I write more. My hands shake.
My tea made too sweet misses my mouth.

Ode to the Decrepit Auction Block
Seen on the Way to My Grandfather's House

The trees won't   stop singing.

       They wrote

                                    ballads of blood.

       They hum

                                    above our heads.

Wind breaks
their branches
like stretched necks.

                Grandfather's house is across the field.
                The magnolias bloom and death sings, too.

                                    Weeds grow in
                                    between its

planks.

                                    It rots next
                                    to cottonwoods.

     What kind

              of trees live

                              near his house?

     What kind

              of songs live

                              in his blood?

Milam and Bryant

Milam: We got an honor code down here.

Bryant: See, we wouldn't have done it if that boy knew his place.

Milam: So we had to show him. You know, teach him a lesson.

Bryant: But he wouldn't shut up.

Milam: He kept crying and begging for his mama.

Bryant: He wouldn't stop.

Milam: So we made him shut up. He can't whistle from under water!

Bryant: We're not murderers, just concerned citizens trying to keep things Right and White. If anything, America owes us an apology.

Milam: Or a thank you.

Bryant: You're welcome, America.

Henry Lee Loggins

i'm haunted

i swear
i swear
i swear

that boy haunts me
when i wake
when i lie down

i swear
i swear

he's here right now

i can't look
in the mirror
and not see
his blood
on my clothes

i tried to tell him
it's not my fault
it was either him
or the both of us
one grave for two black boys

i swear

i would've turned
the gun on myself
if i'd've known
it would be like this

Ode to the River As It Comes Undone

How many bodies have I learned?

    Whether they

        wash themselves in my depths,

            or scream *not it* near my shores,

                or choke until their lungs are full of me,

                    I know them all.

                Water cannot forget.

            It is brought into homes,

        it is cooked with food,

    it consumes.

The Cotton Gin Recalls Emmett

I was born to discard
unwanted parts. With lament

I weighed down
his bullet-hole body.

A silver ring was all that was left
to tell the world he was with me.

A Concerned Citizen Speaks

Minneapolis, Minnesota

May 25th, 1956

To the Editors
Jet Magazine
Chicago, Illinois

Dear sirs,

I was deeply upset with the images you've published. I've never even touched a Negro magazine before, but that photo is all anyone's talking about.

words curdled behind my teeth, the news of that child thick in throat
that child and his beaten face his eyes no longer eyes

It's changed the way that I see my peaceful, all White, community. Were we ever really peaceful?

magazine stale in my fingers index holding the page in place

Generations to come will see this time in history as an embarrassment to White people. But not good White people like me. I assure you, I'm a good White, but I fear you Negros might riot and make even more trouble for yourselves.

tell me I'm a good White I'm afraid of the dark
a future full of Black funerals public executions static on TV screens

After all, your cause can only get so much sympathy.

Sincerely,

A Concerned Citizen

Riddles in the Dark

Q: Why did the Black man cross the road?

A: Because that's where the Klan left his body.

Q: Why do Black folk climb maples?

A: They don't, they only hang from them.

Q: Why don't Black folk go to therapy?

A: There's no need when whiskey exists.

Q: What scares Black folk the most?

A: Open casket funerals.

Q: Why don't Black folk fight back?

A: That's a trick question because it's already a joke.

Wheeler Parker

How could she?

death's to-do list

being black is waking up
one morning then not.
being black is a quickened timer
nailed into your chest.
'have a nice day,' means *'rest in peace'*
or police custody.
whichever comes first.

death relishes its to-do list:

make the bed

                      Breonna Taylor

go for a run

                      Ahmaud Arbery

pay the bills

                      George Floyd

it takes work to keep this body
breathing
when the world says
I breathe too much.

Legion

They call us legion for our own
mouths are muddled. We do not know
which one of us screamed or who severed
our tongues. We cannot speak
of all we have lost.

                        No

                        dead   *stay dead*

Too many stories   of Emmett Till
                        contradict
the   written   imagined   the truth
     replaced

The Jury

We all know they did it,

but

how can we charge
them knowing a ▮▮▮▮▮ boy tried
to tarnish a White woman?

Even if she's married
to that horrid man,
she's a White woman first.

Blood was spilled
when a stern talking-to
would've sufficed,

but

there's only so much
we can excuse.

We're truly sorry
for the boy's family,

but

there's nothing
we can do
knowing
what's been done.

Press Release

We regretfully inform you _____ was shot while _____.
                              (Black person's name)   (existing/saying don't shoot)

The suspect was announced dead upon the arrival of the _____ team.
                                                                (type of social media)

The suspect was _____ and resisting arrest. Witnesses suggested
                (existing/saying don't shoot)

the altercation between officers and _____ was caused by the suspect's
                                     (Black person's name)

_____. The suspect was likely in contact with _____.
(skin color/lack of weapon)   (racial slur, plural)

_____ and other information will be released later this week.
(form of incriminating evidence)

Our hearts go out to _____'s family. Our fine team of officers responded the
                     (Black person's name)

best they knew how in such a stressful situation. No one expected to _____
                                                                                    (murder/be murdered)

that night. We will make sure your concerns are properly _____. An investigat-
                                                                  (exploited/dismissed)

ion is currently in progress. The officers involved were placed on leave and are in

_____ until further notice.
(popular vacation spot)

We truly believe our city is among the greatest in the nation and will not let _____
(racial slur, plural)

take root. Let us unite as Americans in light of this tragedy. Let us use the coming days

to grow even more _____ as a community. Thank you.
(indifferent/undisturbed)

Coon Hunting

Coons tend to stick together,
but all you need is some bait: food,
a coon baby works, too,
if you can catch it. A coon's

been sticking it's head
where it doesn't belong. It keeps
making a mess out of things,
spreading trash all over. If
I'm lucky,

I'll catch a whole bunch of coons.
Wipe out the problem
before more coons start
to notice. I'm just doing

what I have to do.
Those coons won't take over if I have a say!
When I see them up on those oaks with leaves shaking,
they know I know
that's where they belong.

The Noose Undone

Twine tongue your last   embrace

wrapped round boughs I reek of

pale   magnolias   knotted knuckles

                          adore me

my body taut

taunts

those below

                 trade my body   for your dignity

"THE LAW: Trial by Jury," *Time Magazine*, 1955

Sumner, Miss

        a snake-infested swamp

                      of Anglo-American

    traditions

This   system   worse than slavery

        hot and hideous   the white community

            the face of blind hatred

    Bryant and Milam   claimed

            to be

humble

insisted   This whole thing   rigged

                      Mississippi

                 cannot justify   cannot
         jury   Not guilty

Pike County, Mississippi

I. *Ode to Cousins, Almost Forgotten*
Red maples sing your names. Which branches bore your bodies?
Limbs heavy with stolen fruit, your own
limbs tied behind backs, gloves abandoned on the ground
next to a grieving shoe, laces undone,
shined to perfection the night before, your faces
reflect on its ink black shell.

II. *Ode to the Rope Found Near My Grandfather's House*
You've done your job, you artifice.
You, butcher's friend.
You bring ruin.
You, last embrace.

III. *Ode to Flowers*
Divided from dirt, stems are placed into folded hands.
Mouths arranged to hide bloated tongues, perfumed
to disguise decay. Weakened petals fall loose
to prove life is a fugitive. To breathe is to steal.
To exist is to expose.
Even for the lovely. Even for the young.

Inventory of a Black Girl

Model Made: April 27, 1992

Quantity	Item	Details	Value in USD
1	Mouth (full of matches)	Only sulfur can pass through these lips. Only fire is respected. I grow used to swallowed ash.	0
27	Bones (in right hand)	Only useful when made dominant.	0
2	Lungs (full of glass)	When I cough shards come loose & scrape against my teeth.	0

Legion

They called us filth for we were born
　　black like rot. We build
　　our kingdoms in the dirt.

Trees *(noun)*

A plant native to the Americas, *trees* are like graves, except *trees* can grow by themselves.

Used in a sentence:
"Magnolia trees are a pastoral scene of the gallant south"
"That tree across town has the best pears. But after last summer, I won't go near it."

Synonyms: uncle, cousin, brother

Interview with Carolyn Bryant on the Anniversary of Emmett's Death

Carolyn Bryant did only one known interview.

Carolyn Bryant: What am I supposed to talk about?

Interviewer: How would you explain the South to a ▮▮▮▮ who's never visited before?

Bryant: (*Laughs*) Questions like that might get you in trouble!

Interviewer: Pretend you're writing up an etiquette guide so ▮▮▮ won't get in trouble. Just talk to me like you would any one of your friends.

Bryant: You think I don't know what day today is? Like I could ever forget what happened last year? (*Takes deep breath*) We Southerners can tell when someone's not from around here before they even speak. Especially ▮▮▮▮. The secret is, when you look at them and size them up, see if they look back. Them ▮▮▮▮▮ look right back at you, all wide-eyed, like you the one acting funny. Some of the bolder ones might even try to talk to you. Those uppity ▮▮▮ got the nerve to shake they heads at you, like they might really do something. That's when you know they don't know our ways. Those ▮▮▮ don't last very long in the South.

The ▮▮▮ around here know better than that. Most of them, that is. The ones that can't leave well enough alone usually leave after seeing how we do things down here. Sometimes they have to leave in the dead of night, but that's their fault for starting shit in the first place.

Every so often you have to teach ▮▮▮▮ a lesson, or use one as a lesson for other ▮▮▮ to stay in their place. Sometimes, it feels like the only way we can really have peace is if we string one up every now and then.

▮▮▮ make trouble, ▮▮▮ get trouble.

Same goes for those ▮▮▮▮▮ coming down here trying to help folks that don't need to be helped. Why can't they see they're the ones giving us Southerners a bad name? Every time one of them starts some kind of sit-in, or protest, or whatever's the latest fashion up there, they put ideas in the good good ▇▇ heads that what they have ain't good enough. Then those ▇▇▇▇ start thinking they can do the same thing as the bad ones, then they all start acting like they ain't got no sense, then blood is spilled when they all could've just kept quiet.

Even if the ▇▇▇▇▇▇▇▇ look white as can be, the real Southerners among us know that they're just ▇▇▇▇ turned inside out. And they have to learn their lesson, too. Just like the ▇▇▇.

We have a joke down here that the reason why our food is so fresh is because ▇▇▇▇ make wonderful fertilizer. At least the dirt has made good use of them.

"The Shocking Story of Approved Killing in Mississippi," *Look Magazine,* 1956

        editors   convinced
of
            myth   exposed

                                poison

                Milam   Bryant

                          perfect
martyrdom
    bastards   afraid of

                                a ------   a
few   ------

      that poison
                                an example
of

                  white
    satisfaction

Moses Wright

I've stopped asking why. All it takes
is asking the wrong person. I tried telling
Emmett that. They can shame you.
Beat you within an inch of your life.
But don't you ever ask why. I told him
to apologize faster than he could breathe. Maybe
he did and they just felt like killing. Maybe
it never occurred to them to ask why they'd want
to. I'll never get the answers I need, even if I did know
                                                                                         why.

Jet **Magazine Staff**

For immediate release:

When Ms. Till first asked that we publish pictures of her dead son we thought she was out of her mind. What kind of respectable magazine would print photos of a child's mangled corpse? We encouraged her to write nice eulogy, or even to find a magazine more willing to show violence this out of control. But we realized that was the point—to show how this violence is out of control. The judge, the town, the entire world, it seems, is out of their minds. The world must know. Emmett's story must be told right.

"Historian recalls moment Emmett's accuser admitted she lied," *CBS News*, 2017

    white woman

                                      silence

is

                a

burden   to

                                        witness

To Be Soft

My grandmother's hands were like figs
dried in a Mississippi summer. Her scars read like love notes:
calluses born in cotton fields, mason jar lid imprints
on her palms, freckled pricks from needles left
in purses, burns near her right wrist.
She was slow with chicken grease.

Sometimes she'd lather dishes and scrub the same cup
until its shine rivaled finery seen
in the Sears catalogs she loved to keep.

She dreamt of mansions up north filled with linen
only meant for others to envy. Her help
would press stubborn shirts and fetch
her coat if the wind even whispered of frost.
They'd rub lavender on her hands until she was soft
as watered earth.

They'd clean windows for her to watch lesser women
pass by, their hands rough like cracked dirt. Thoughts
fixed on to-do list, their own overseers.

A Subtle Truth / Self Portrait as a Chair

Black boy pain is the only ache
worth being pain

                                        consistently stepped
                                        on for others
                                        to reach higher places,

Black girl pain just is pain
Black boy pain is more than pain

                                        not useful

                                        when missing screws.
                                        utility based
                                        solely on activity

is the only pain worth being pain
is more than pain is pain on Black girl Black girl pain

                                        often seen
                                        in certain spaces
                                        (a kitchen, an office,
                                        sometimes outside
                                        if the ground isn't good
                                        enough).

is pain on pain on pain Black girl pain
is plain as Black girl pain plain to see on Black girl

Black girl pain is Black girl
plain Black girl in pain

                                        tends to shake
                                        if under too much pressure.

Black girl pain
is worth less than Black girl

Black girl worth less in pain
Black girl pain is worthless to Black boy pain

is worth to Black girl
worthless pain is Black girl pain

is worth to Black girl
Black boy pain is the only pain
$\qquad\qquad\qquad\qquad$ in frequent need
$\qquad\qquad\qquad\qquad$ of repair.

pain is worse to Black girl
Black pain is girl

4
To the girls of the 16th Street Baptist Church bombing

I.
What better place to plant
a bomb than under church steps?
Four girls in choir robes
thrown through stained glass.

II.
Four killers called to court
in their Sunday suits.
A quick slap on the wrist,
their smiles intact.

III.
Their lives a prize
for hooded knights.
IV.
These bodies,
these blessed bodies,
trapped in brick,
too burned to turn cold.

The Train Gives Birth
From the 63rd St Station in Chicago, IL to Money, Mississippi

Belly pregnant with cargo, limbs drag
across wooden planks. Diesel poured
into my mouth, thick and sticky.
Smoke catches in my throat.

Across wooden planks, diesel is poured
on expecting hands. My lifeblood.
Throats catch smoke,
each cough a movement forward.

Expecting hands fumble my lifeblood.
I take what's mine.
Each cough a movement forward,
bodies birthed a new existence.

I take what's mine.
I've mothered many through this passage.
Bodies birthed a new existence,
no way to keep them safe.

I've mothered many through this passage.
They exit the womb at their stations,
no safety to keep.
Seats no longer reserved.

They exit the womb at their stations.
What becomes of my sucklings?
Seats no longer reserved.
Pregnant belly drags cargo.

"Why Are We Still Reliving the Nightmarish Death of Emmett Till?" *The Nation*, 2016

The Till trial

"not guilty" verdict   a foregone conclusion

the   white race

desperate

to survive

black lives matter

controversial

white nationalists

nourish the illusion   of   European innocence   a state
applicable to the Trumpian world of today

a national nightmare   unable to awake

The Only Black Kid at the Punk Show

After Kevin Young's "On Being the Only Black Person at the Johnny Paycheck Concert"

The girl in the Green Day shirt
wants to touch my hair. *It looks so soft*, she says.

I inch towards a pack of boys
with multi-colored mohawks like mixed drinks
they're too young to have; a boy briefly looks
at me before returning to his conversation
on how Courtney killed Kurt Cobain.

She's head of the Illuminati, he says with conviction—
conspiracy theories laid out like a buffet
for his friends to consume.

The merch booth behind me sells band shirts
that are almost antique. Suburban kids
pass gossip around like flavored vape pens
and block the way to the bathroom.

The band enters the stage. The crowd sways,
an ocean of salty skin under a shelter of speakers.
I stand in the back, an outcast,

not old enough to reminisce
when Black rock stars were as common as record players.
When rock 'n' roll just meant the blues,
when blues just meant wicked songs
dipped in gospel, when Black was just

the rule to be in rock. I'm just a kid born too Black
to rebel with rap bleeding
from headphones. Too Black

to know *Nevermind* by heart.
My heart, black and bleeding, ripped
from my body and thrown on stage.
The band throws it to the crowd
saying, *I love you all, you're too kind.*

Legion

We named ourselves Legion
to make us many. Our willows grow only themselves,
not ruined men. We, once hunted, live on land
that loves us back.

Praise be the Planters

My ancestors braided seeds
into their hair as they were stored
on forbidden ships.

As I write this poem on a park bench,
seeds kiss my hair and fall on the page.
I know this is a shared vocabulary
across oceans, across generations,
and other measures of time:

how long it takes
for a wave to reach the shore,
how long it takes
for rings to multiply beneath bark,
how long it takes for me to realize

when I haven't taken a breath. My lungs a reminder
that I'm a dream made real, a seed released.

Repurposed Litany

Let us praise how we've thrived under war.
We've made things that tried to kill us into fields
of sunflowers, gardenias, orchids, and marigolds.

When the wind whips leaves
from forest, friends we lost enchant
our ears saying, "We will come back."

Those used to safety discard plants with scars,
but it's our grandmothers' speaking, "We are still here."
This is why dirt has color.

We are born cultivators.

When our grandmothers passed we grew
in their place. Let us praise how their gardens
sing us home.

Notes

The epigraph on page 1 is from Timothy B. Tyson's book, *The Blood of Emmett Till* (Simon & Schuster, 2017).

The "Legion" poem on page 3 starts with a quote from Mark 5:9 (NIV).

Page 16 is inspired by an interview with Emmett's cousin, Wheeler Parker, conducted by Joseph Mosier through the Library of Congress. www.loc.gov/item/2015669110/

Page 25 is an erasure poem of an excerpt from the 1955 *Time* Magazine article, "THE LAW: Trial by Jury." http://content.time.com/time/subscriber/article/0,33009,807680-3,00.html

Page 30 contains a quote from the song "Strange Fruit," written by Abel Meerpol and performed by Billie Holiday.

The epigraph on page 31 is based on information from Timothy B. Tyson's book, *The Blood of Emmett Till*, which is the only interview Carolyn Bryant ever gave.

Page 33 is an erasure poem of an excerpt from the *LOOK Magazine* article by William Bradford Huie. http://www.pbs.org/wgbh/americanexperience/features/till-killers-confession/

Page 36 is an erasure of a 2017 CBS News article, "Historian Recalls Moment Emmett's Accuser Admitted She Lied." https://www.cbsnews.com/news/the-blood-of-emmett-till-carolyn-bryant-lied-timothy-tyson-new-book/
See also: Tyson's book, *The Blood of Emmett Till*

Page 43 is an erasure poem of an excerpt from a 2016 *The Nation* article, "Why Are We Still Reliving the Nightmarish Death of Emmett Till?," by Dan Wakefield. http://thenation.com/article/why-are-we-still-reliving-the-nightmarish-death-of-emmett-till/

Page 44 contains a quote from the Kevin Young poem, "On Being the Only Black Person at the Johnny Paycheck Concert."

Page 45 contains a quote from Danez Smith's poem, "summer, somewhere."

Acknowledgments

Thank you to the literary journals who published versions of the poems in this book.

Anomaly: "Walthall County, Mississippi," "Press Release," and "Trees (Noun)"

AGNI: "The Slave's Descendant Addresses King Cotton"

Cola Literary Review: "Ode to the Decrepit Auction Block Seen on the Way to My Grandfather's House"

LandLocked: "Pike County, Mississippi"

Aquifer: "Inventory of a Black Girl"

diode poetry journal: "To Be Soft"

The Indianapolis Review: "A Subtle Truth / Self Portrait as a Chair"

Booth: "The Only Black Kid at the Punk Show"

There are so many people that helped bring this book into existence. These shout outs, however unorthodox, are a small token of my thanks.

Thank you, God, for blessing me with the book. Baby Chevy wouldn't believe all the things that you've made happen.

To my Mom for coming to all of my shows. Thank you, Dad, for trusting me with your stories.

Thanks, Kiana, for your support. To Aniyah—when you're old enough to read this I hope that TT Chevy has made you proud.

To Grandpa, Grandma, and Granny. To my ancestors before them. I am because you were.

To my many aunts, uncles, and cousins for giving me a full spectrum of Blackness and for helping me figure myself out.

To Sun Yung Shin—this book wouldn't be a book without you. I'm eternally grateful that you saw talent in me when I couldn't see it myself.

To Halee Kirkwood for the invaluable feedback and friendship.

To Beau Rara—my life is so much better with you around.

Thank you, Amirah Ellison, for being my family and making me sound smart.

To Victoria Lin Peterson-Hilleque for your endless creativity and our monthly adventures.

Thank you, Celina McManus, for the adjunct camaraderie and commiseration.

To Ruo Gan for liking my playlists and loving me fully.

Thank you, Kathryn Melendez, for teaching me accountability and how to keep fighting the fight.

Thank you, Mollie Wetherall, for your help during my darker times.

To Melinda Lee and the rest of 2018 Queer Trans Indigenous People of Color conference team. We really did reclaim our magic that weekend!

To Pastor Tyler Sit and literally everyone at New City Church. Y'all keep me sane.

Thank you, *Alternating Current Press*, for being the first people to ever publish me.

Thank you, McKnight Foundation, The Loft Literary Center, and the Given Foundation for American American Literature for the space you make for artists. A special shout out is owed to the 2016-2017 Loft Mentor Series and the 2016 Givens cohort for giving me my start.

To Sagirah Shahid and Maya Beck—my siblings. I have so much love for you both.

To Maggie DeSmet and Brad Harris—you saved me. Thank you.

To Frankie Gomez—the Pete Wentz to my Patrick, the John Lennon to my Paul.

Thank you, James Everest, for constantly pushing my definition of art.

To Jason Thomas and the other Carleton Liberal Arts Experience '08 babies! It was easily one of the best weeks of my teenage life.

To David Cruz, my favorite philosopher.

To Steve Bigboy and Kelvin Peprah, the de facto godfathers to my nonexistent children.

Thank you, Lindsey Reuer, for the absolutely epic mixed CDs and for being the friend my childhood self dreamed that I would have someday.

To the writers who raised me: Lucille Clifton, Tyehimba Jess, Kevin Young, Eion Colfer, David Levithan, Ai, Cornelius Eady, Gwendolyn Brooks, Alice Walker, Toni Morrison, W. E. B. Du Bois.

To Gen Del Raye—I've always loved your stories.

Thank you D. Allen, Merle Geode, and Lior for reminding me that my body and its stories are sacred.

To April Gibson for being one of the realest people I know.

To Liz Kaufman who inspires me to be better.

To Hillary Barbetta. You mean so much to me.

Thank you, Thet-Htar Thet, and everyone who has ever taken my Reclaiming Language or American Mythology classes.

To Lauren Chow for keeping me grounded.

To Blanca Crespin and Erin Geyen—I wouldn't have survived grad school without you two.

Thank you, Village Parks, Marius, and Nacho for giving me something to look forward to all of those Tuesday nights.

To Rebecca Song for being so fucking cool.

To Alice Paige for all of the car rides, deep conversations, and delicious chai.

Thank you to the many teachers and mentors that I've had: Abdul Ali, Katrina Vandenberg, Douglas Kearney, Anna Meek, Patricia Smith, Keri Asp, Greg Hewitt, Deborah Keenan, Danez Smith, Lesley Arimah, Matt Mauch, Gretchen Marquette, Matt Rasmussen, Delania Haug, Kari Slade, Angela and Richard Pelster-Wiebe. To my first grade teacher, Ms. Stone, for encouraging me to write in the first place.

To Upstream Arts for supporting me as an artist and employee.

Thank you, Jade Yueng. I'm so grateful that our paths crossed.

Thank you, Michael Kleber-Diggs, for your brilliant mind and infectious humor.

To my 2018 Tin House Winter Workshop crew: Jody Chan, Jay Ward, Lucy Burns, Arriel Vinson, Shakthi Sharma, and our fearless leader, Erica Dawson.

Thank you to my 2023 Bread Loafers, especially Patrick Phillips and our workshop group.

To Jen Bowen, Mike Alberti, Su Hwang, and all the instructors at the Minnesota Prison Writing Workshop. To our students—you make this work worth it.

To Sam Stokley—who lets me be my messy self.

To Peter Limthongviratn for making me look good and the awesome photos.

To Julian Calavera for turning my poems into visual art and for making the bomb cover for the book.

To my treatment team: Renita Wilson, Alford Karayusuf, Kate McTavish, and Lindsey Brumm. To the friends I made at summer camp. Thank you L. B. and R. P. for your support.

Thank you, Roy G. Guzmán and LM Brimmer, for the group chats, Zoom dates, and coffee meet ups.

Thank you, Jen Manthey, for your kind and genuine spirit.

To Amy Blickensderfer for reminding me to stay in my body and for all of the dance lessons.

To Anthony Ceballos, my favorite co-host.

Thanks to the musicians who taught me how to write long before I picked up any poetry book: Fall Out Boy, Bright Eyes, Relient K, U2, Arctic Monkeys, Sufjan Stevens, Switchfoot, Margot & The Nuclear So And So's, and Gorillaz.

Thank you to the musicians that kept me company when writing: boygenius, Hozier, Frank Ocean, Louie Zong, Janelle Monáe, grentperez, and the Marcus Hedge Orchestra with their amazing *Adventure Time* covers. Thanks also to Rebecca Sugar and Pendleton Ward for the shows they created.

To the people at Finishing Line Press for taking a chance on my manuscript.

To Jay Shen. I love you beyond words.

I could go on for days thanking the many, many, people who made me a writer, but this is where I'll stop. If I've forgotten anyone please know that it's my own shortsightedness rather than you lacking meaning to me.

To you, dear reader. Thank you, thank you, thank you.

Chavonn Williams Shen (she/they) is from Minneapolis, Minnesota. She was a 2022 McKnight Writing fellow and a first runner-up for *The Los Angeles Review* Flash Fiction Contest. She was also a Best of the Net Award finalist, a Pushcart Prize nominee, a winner of the Loft Literary Center's Mentor Series, a fellow with the Givens Foundation for African American Literature, and an instructor for the Minnesota Prison Writing Workshop. A Bread Loaf, Tin House, VONA, and Hurston/Wright workshop alum, her writing has appeared in: *Diode Poetry Journal, Anomaly, AGNI,* and others. *Still Life with Rope and River* is her debut book.

www.ingramcontent.com/pod-product-compliance
Lightning Source LLC
Chambersburg PA
CBHW020342170426
43200CB00006B/480